Pe

in c

and other stories

Marie Birkinshaw

Lorraine Horsley

Shirley Jackson

Mandy Ross

Written by:

Marie Birkinshaw	(pp.5–7, 34–37)
Shirley Jackson	(pp.12–13, 14–17, 28–30, 31–33, 38–39)
Mandy Ross	(pp.4, 8–11, 18–20, 21–23, 24–27, 40–42, 43–46, 47–48)

Illustrated by:

Garry Davies	(pp.4, 5–7, 14–17, 38–39, 47–48)
Jon Davis	(pp.12–13, 18–20)
Patricia Ludlow	(pp.8–11)
Sebastian Palmer	(pp.31–33)
Peter Stevenson	(pp.21–23, 28–30, 43–46)
Sean Longcroft	(pp.24–27, 34–37, 40–42)

Cover illustration by Garry Davies

Designed by Heather Blackham

Project Co-ordinator: Fran Stevens

Published by BASS publications 2005
Martineau Centre, Balden Road,
Harborne, Birmingham B32 2EH

ISBN: 1-898244-98-7

Contents

Penguins in a spin

What's black and white and can see at night?

A penguin with a torch.

What's black and white and good to eat?

A penguin's biscuit.

Trying it on

Do you want these new shoes?
But I like my old ones.

Do you want these new shoes?
Yes! They are just like my old ones.

Teamwork

Our team takes more paper than their team.

What a lot of paper!
Paper here

Our team takes more paint than their team.

What a lot of paint!
Paint here

Our team takes longer than their team.

But our plane stays up longer than their plane!

Great plane!
What a great plane!

Mum and me

"You can't go out like that," said Mum.

"You can't go out like that," I said.

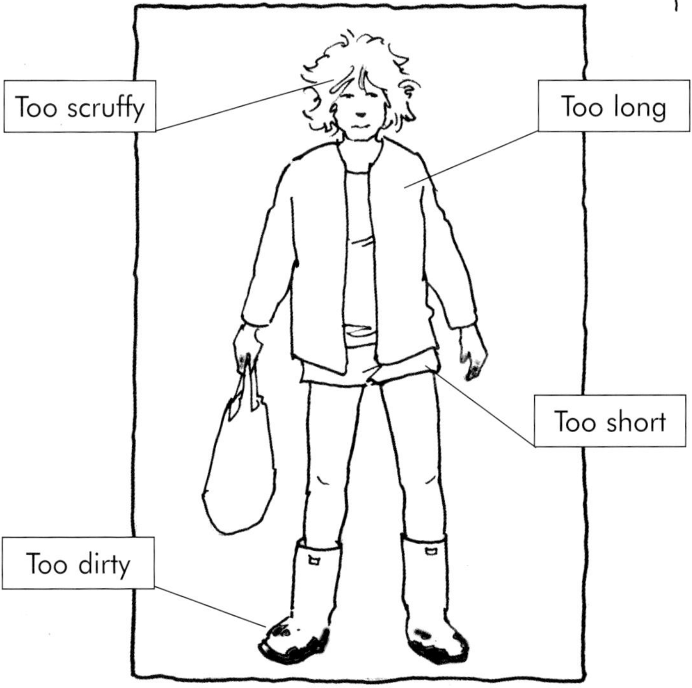

Calling home

Dad went away. I called him.
"Come home, Dad," I said.

"I can't," said Dad.

I called him again.
"Come home, Dad," I said.

"I can't," said Dad.

I called him again.
"Come home, Dad," I said.

"I can't," said Dad.

"I'm home!" called Dad.

"But I'm not!"

Very odd numbers

What has nine feet?

Three aliens have nine feet.

What has eleven feet?

Two dogs and an alien have eleven feet.

What has thirteen feet?

Three aliens and a dog
have thirteen feet.

What has fifteen feet?

Five aliens have fifteen feet.

What has seventeen feet?

Four dogs and a pirate have seventeen feet.

What has nineteen feet?

Three aliens, two dogs and two pirates have nineteen feet.

A maths play

20 - 12 = ?
A maths play for two people
Naj: Can you do this one? Twenty take away twelve is...
Liz: Um... eight.

Liz: You do the next one. Twenty take away eight is...
Naj: Um... twelve. Look! It adds up!
Liz: Yes! So twelve add eight makes...
Naj: Twenty. See! It all adds up.
20 - 12 = 8...
20 - 8 = 12...
8 + 12 = 20...
Good work!

Liz: What's next? Eighteen take away four is…
18 - 4 = ?
Naj: Um… fourteen.
Liz: So eighteen take away fourteen is…
Naj: Four. So four and fourteen make…
Liz: Eighteen. See! It all adds up.
4 + 14 = 18!

Training for the team

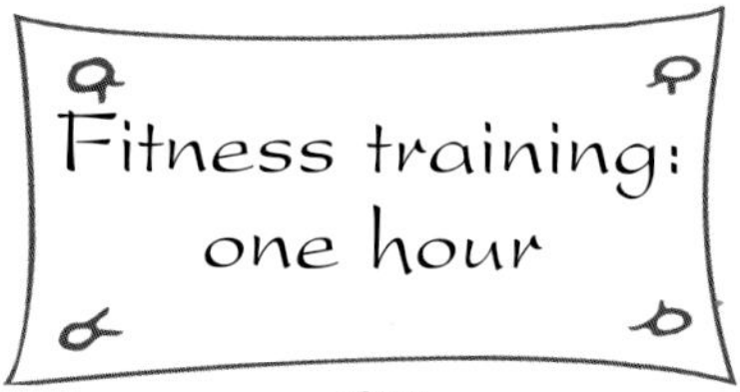

I spent fourteen minutes climbing...

sixteen minutes walking...

thirteen minutes jumping and seventeen minutes swimming.

Football training:
one hour

I spent eleven minutes
running with the ball...

nineteen minutes running
from side to side...

eighteen minutes on the side and
twelve minutes cheering sixteen goals!

I spent sixteen minutes in the bath...

four minutes getting dressed...

eight minutes
eating pizza...

half an hour
watching television...

two minutes
running up
to bed...

and then I
spent twelve
hours sleeping.
Zzzzzzz

Who lives at...?

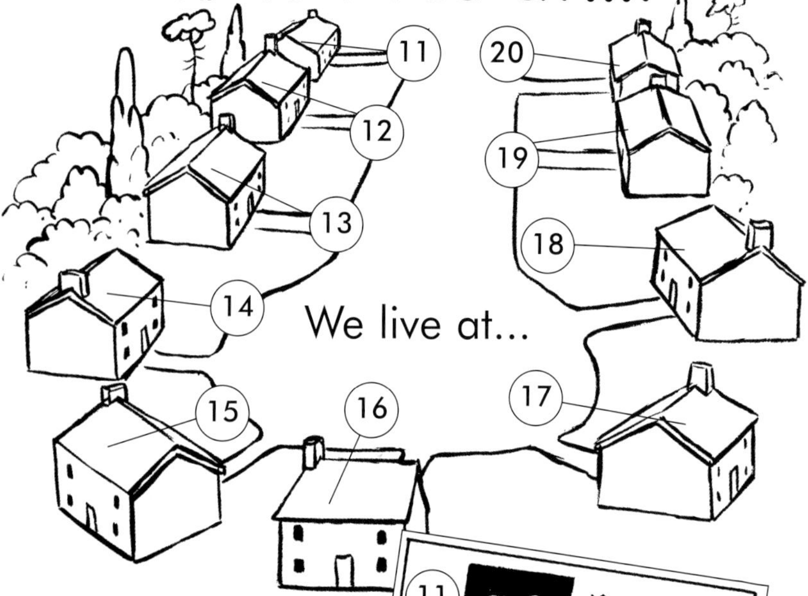

Number Eleven
Gran
Grandad
Grandson

Number Twelve
Mum
Boyfriend
Little boy
Little girl

Number Thirteen
Mum
Baby
Cat

Number Fourteen
Dad
Mum
Little girl

Number Fifteen
Mum
Dad
Brother
Sister
Baby sister
Dog

Number Sixteen
Dad
Girlfriend
Baby

Number Seventeen
Gran
Mum
Brother
Sister

Number Eighteen
Boyfriend
Girlfriend
Cat

Number Nineteen
Gran
Grandad
Dog

Number Twenty
Mum
Dad
Brother
Baby brother

Cool stuff

Where's that from?
Where did you get it?
Where's that from?
Can I try it on?

Where's that from?
Where did you get it?
Where's that from?
Can I have a go?

Where's that from?
Where did you get it?
Where's that from?
Can I have a look?

Here it is,
have a look.

Cool!

Doctor, doctor

On Monday I went to see the doctor.
"You must get fit," he said.

So... on Tuesday I played football.

On Wednesday
I went swimming.

On Thursday
I played tennis.

On Friday
I played cricket.

On Saturday I played basketball.

On Sunday I played football and tennis and cricket and basketball, and **then** I went swimming.

On Monday I went to see the doctor again.

"**Wow!**" said the doctor. "How did you do it?"

Bad hair day

Monday: This is a bad hair day.

Tuesday: This is a very bad hair day.

Wednesday:
This is a very, very bad hair day.

Thursday: This is not so bad.
Friday: This is good.
Saturday: This is very good.
Sunday: This is a very, very good hair day!
SPORT

The name code

We have a code. It is a name code.

In our code, his name is Den.

In our code, his name is Mot.

In our code, her name is Zil.

What is your name?
My name is Pip.
In our code, your name is... uh-oh! In our code your name is... Pip!

Have you seen...?

"Have you seen my bag?" said Mum.
"I may have... or I may not," I said.

"Have you seen my keys?" said Mum.
"I may have... or I may not," I said.

"Have you seen my glasses?" said Mum.
"I may have... or I may not," I said.

"Have you seen this chocolate?"
said Mum.

"May I have some?" I said.
"YOU MAY NOT!" said Mum.

Penguins in a spin again

What's black and white and has four wheels?

A penguin on a skateboard.

What are black and white and go up and down?

Penguins on a yo-yo.

What's black and white and goes round and round?

Help!
washing machine

A penguin in a washing machine!

What's pink and black and white and goes round and round?

Help! Help!
Help! Help!

A pig and a penguin in a washing machine!